A Guide to Safe Practice in Art & Design

London: HMSO

Department for Education
Sanctuary Buildings
Great Smith Street
London SW1P 3BT
0171 925 5000

ISBN 0 11 270896 X

Contents

1 Introduction

As with any practical activity, there is an element of risk in art and design activities. However, this can be kept to an acceptable minimum if those involved are aware of the potential hazards and take appropriate steps to avoid accidents. It is particularly important that teachers are aware of their responsibilities regarding health and safety and ensure that pupils act safely, within acceptable bounds, at all times. This guide is intended primarily for secondary school teachers who are responsible for practical activities in art and design. General class teachers in primary schools, lecturers in further, higher and adult education, and those training to be teachers may also find it helpful.

Although some local authorities provide guidelines to the schools they maintain on health and safety in art and design activities, not all do. There are few readily accessible, up-to-date publications for teachers which deal exclusively with the subject.

The purpose of this guide is to draw together the range of health and safety issues affecting art and design activities and, more specifically, to highlight the legal duties arising from health and safety legislation introduced over the last few years. This places various responsibilities on local authorities, schools and teachers designed generally to ensure the safety and well-being of employees and those in their care. This guide draws attention to particular areas where accidents commonly occur and provides examples of good practice to help avoid such incidents.

The guide is not intended to inhibit the teaching of art and design. Teachers may feel that their freedom to carry out some activities is constrained by recent safety legislation. However, the purpose of such legislation is rarely to ban activities but rather to ensure that they are carried out in a safe and efficient manner. This guide aims to clarify the position on what is permitted and encourage good, safe practice in art and design.

This booklet cannot provide a complete guide to all the potential specific hazards and safety procedures relating to materials, equipment and methods which might be used in art and design. Its main purpose is to help teachers be more aware of the inherent risks, and to encourage the seeking of further specialist advice if the information available in this publication is insufficient. A detailed reference list of further information sources is included at the back of the guide.

The Department for Education wishes to thank the National Society for Education in Art and Design (NSEAD) for their work on this publication.

2 Relevant Legislation

Employers and staff have legal responsibilities concerning health and safety under both common and statute law. The main regulations and requirements which have implications for the management and organisation of practical activities in schools are set out below. Other relevant legislation and guidance referred to elsewhere in the text is listed in section 8.

2.1 Common Law

There are long-established and important common law requirements for those acting in loco parentis to exercise the same care as a reasonable parent would in the same circumstances. Those in charge of children should be aware of the school's health and safety policy (see section 2.2.2) and the appropriate action to take in the event of an accident or emergency.

2.2 Statute Law

2.2.1 Health and Safety at Work etc Act (1974)

Under the Health and Safety at Work etc Act (HSWA), employers are required to do all that is reasonably practicable to ensure the health, safety and welfare at work of employees, and the health and safety of non-employees affected by their duties such as pupils and visitors. In LEA-maintained schools the employer is the local education authority. In voluntary-aided and self-governing (grant-maintained) schools the employer is the governing body. In most independent schools the employer is the proprietor.

As a result of the European Commission's programme of action on health and safety, a number of new regulations came into force on 1 January 1993. There were several new requirements, but the regulations primarily sought to clarify and make more explicit current health and safety law. Although some of the following regulations relate only to employers and employees, the Health and Safety Executive (HSE) would expect employers to regard these requirements as a reasonable standard to be applied to pupils.

2.2.2 The Management of Health and Safety at Work Regulations (1992)

These regulations require employers to introduce arrangements for planning, organising, controlling, monitoring and reviewing their management of health and safety. Such arrangements should include the production of written assessments of risks to which employees, pupils and others might be exposed. Employees should be provided with information on these measures and should receive suitable health and safety training. To achieve effective health and safety management, employers and staff should work together to produce a sound health and safety policy for the school.

2.2.3 Control of Substances Hazardous to Health (COSHH) Regulations (1994)

These regulations are among the most important since the HSWA (1974).

They place a duty on employers to make an assessment of risks for work with toxic and corrosive substances hazardous to health, and to take necessary steps to prevent or control adequately the exposure of employees to these substances. In addition to the materials used in art and design, and dust created by practical work, attention should be paid to the potentially harmful effects from work with cleaning agents. Care should always be taken when using such products.

Although the principal legal responsibility rests with the employer, employees also have specific duties to make full and proper use of control measures and personal protective equipment, and to report all defects.

2.2.4   The Workplace (Health, Safety and Welfare) Regulations (1992)

These regulations concern the working environment, safety, facilities and cleaning of the workplace and are applicable only to employees. However, they affect pupils insofar as they share much of the school environment with teachers or other employees.

Consideration should be given to the design of work areas with reference to room dimensions and space; layout of areas to allow 'traffic routes'; safe storage; provision for the disabled; sufficient natural lighting in machine areas; and interior walls and ceilings which can easily be cleaned.

2.2.5   The Personal Protective Equipment at Work Regulations (1992)

These regulations set out sound principles for selecting, providing, maintaining and using personal protective equipment (PPE) designed to be worn or held to minimise risks to health or safety. Employers must ensure that suitable clothing is provided for employees at risk, and that it is adequately maintained and stored appropriately. Employees are required to use equipment in accordance with their training and instructions, and must report any defect in their PPE. Schools should take these requirements into consideration when preparing risk assessments for pupils involved in work where the need for PPE arises.

Only PPE with the approved 'CE' (Communauté Européenne) mark should be purchased. PPE should always be stored correctly. Employers need to provide PPE for each employee (pupils and teachers) who may be exposed to risks. Information and training in the use of PPE should be provided.

2.2.6   The Provision and Use of Work Equipment Regulations (1992)

This legislation places general duties on employers to deal with selected hazards, and also lists minimum requirements for work equipment. The regulations apply to all equipment, ranging from hand-tools to complex machinery, and its use.

The duties require the provision of suitable equipment, taking account of the purposes for which it will be used; the conditions and hazards of the workplace; maintenance requirements to ensure that it is kept in good working order; and the provision of adequate training. Specific requirements include guards for dangerous parts of machinery, control systems and devices, isolation from the source of energy, lighting, stability and hazard warnings.

2.2.7   The Health and Safety (Display Screen Equipment) Regulations (1992)

These regulations apply only to display screens used by a worker for a significant part of the day. Although the risk for such users is generally thought not to be high, it can arguably lead to muscular and other physical problems, eye strain and mental stress.

The implications for art and design are likely to be minimal, since prolonged use of computers and visual display units (VDUs) is not common in this context. However, attention is increasingly drawn to potential hazards. For example, concerns have been expressed about the distance between user and screen, the possible effects of very low-frequency radiation from the screen and adjacent work stations, eye disorders, and physical discomfort such as back strain and other posture-related stresses.

Employers also have duties to ensure that work stations satisfy requirements concerning the equipment itself, furniture and working environment. Breaks must be planned and information and training provided for users. Although the regulations relate to employers and employees, the HSE's own guidance is particularly useful when considering risk assessments for pupils using VDUs.

2.2.8   The Electricity at Work Regulations (1989)

These regulations place a duty on employers to ensure that electrical installations and equipment are in safe working order. Employees are required to co-operate with their employers in meeting the requirements of the regulations.

2.2.9   The Manual Handling Operations Regulations (1992)

These regulations concern the lifting or moving of heavy loads, and affect both employers and employees. Employers are required to take appropriate steps to reduce the risk involved in manual handling and to provide employees with information about the weight of each load. Employees should comply with these instructions.

2.2.10   The Highly Flammable Liquids and Liquefied Petroleum Gases Regulations (1972)

As these regulations are made under the Factories Act (1961) they do not apply to schools. However, the regulations relating to the storage of highly flammable liquids (HFLs) with a flashpoint under 32°C are regarded as setting standards which must be met by schools in order to conform with the HSWA.

Employers must ensure that HFLs are stored appropriately and that store rooms, bins or cupboards are suitably marked.

2.2.11   The Health and Safety (Signs and Signals) Regulations (1995)

Employers are required to display a safety sign wherever there is a risk to health. Existing safety signs complying with the 1980 regulations are acceptable. As far as schools are concerned, new signs relating to fire-fighting equipment are being introduced, and there is also a requirement to display signs on stores if significant quantities of dangerous substances are kept.

Further information about this regulation is available from the Health and Safety Executive (HSE).

2.2.12 Reporting of Injuries, Diseases and Dangerous Occurrences Regulations (RIDDOR) (1985)

Major injuries occurring on school premises should be reported to the HSE in accordance with these regulations. In addition to being of statistical value, the information is used to determine whether a visit from a member of the HSE Inspectorate is necessary.

2.3 Recording Accidents

Although pupils are not covered by the Health and Safety (First Aid) Regulations (1981), which relate to employees, those acting in loco parentis have a general duty of care. Pupils' first aid needs should also be protected by the school's health and safety first aid and medical policy, which should ensure that the school has an appropriate number of qualified first aiders among the staff.

It is recommended that schools maintain an independent record of all incidents and accidents, however minor, in accordance with the local authority's instructions or, in the case of self-governing (grant-maintained) and independent schools, along similar lines to the Social Services record of accidents to employees (Form BI 510). Data from the accident book provides a valuable source of information to be considered in the assessment of risks in accordance with the Management of Health and Safety at Work Regulations.

2.4 Teachers' Legal Responsibilities

Teachers and other employees must take reasonable care for ensuring their own health and safety and that of their colleagues and pupils. They must also cooperate with their employers to enable them to comply with their duties under the HSWA (1974). It is important that health and safety requirements are met and that advice and instructions from governors, headteachers or the local authority are always followed. Unsafe practices and conditions must be reported to the employer. Given their general management responsibilities, it is likely that headteachers and heads of departments will undertake greater responsibility than other staff for health and safety matters.

The Management of Health and Safety at Work Regulations (1992) impose a duty on employers to ensure that their establishments are safe and healthy places. Those in charge of children have a common law responsibility in loco parentis to look after children in their care and ensure they do not come to harm. Teachers are therefore expected to exercise the same degree of care which a careful parent would take in the same circumstances.

In law, employers are generally responsible for the negligence of their employees when such action has resulted in injury to another person. If legal action is brought, it is possible for a teacher to be named separately, particularly if the negligence was during an activity not reasonably regarded as a requirement of the employer. However, when staff do accept special responsibilities it does not necessarily follow that they are personally liable for the consequences of any accident. In the event of legal action, if negligence is proven, a court might decide that the teacher had been given inadequate training or that the delegation of responsibility was inappropriate.

Teachers who are in any doubt about the extent of their responsibility may wish to check their position with their employer or professional association.

2.5 Risk Assessments

Employers are required under the Management of Health and Safety at Work Regulations (1992) to undertake an assessment of risks in the work place. In schools, this function may be delegated to the headteacher or head of department. There is a clearly defined process which must be followed in carrying out a risk assessment, including:

- identifying the hazards
- assessing the risks
- assigning priority to the risks
- deciding whether they are properly controlled or whether further action is needed
- making a written record of the assessment.

In practice, a risk assessment is nothing more than a careful examination of what in the school could cause harm to pupils or staff. In the art and design department you will need to decide whether you have taken sufficient precautions to avoid accidents or whether further preventative measures need to be introduced. Reasonable steps should be taken to ensure that potential hazards are removed and risks are controlled to minimise the likelihood of harm to staff and pupils. Once the examination of hazards and risks has been carried out you must record your findings, including how the assessment was done, what checks were made, how hazards were dealt with, what precautions were taken, and what further action may be necessary.

If you are unsure about what to do, local health and safety inspectors can provide further advice on legal requirements and safety standards.

3 Safety Education

Teachers may understandably become anxious when confronted with the apparent complexities of health and safety legislation, and consequently may feel that they must limit the range of activities they undertake with children. Normal classroom practice in art and design need not be unduly restricted because of fears about health and safety. Normal practices are safe, within the acceptable bounds of risk-taking.

Pupils should be aware that controlling health and safety risks is an essential part of everyday life. Although the primary responsibility for the school's health and safety policy rests with the employer, it is just as important that managers and all employees clearly recognise their roles and legal responsibilities. Pupils and visitors also have a duty under the HSWA not intentionally or recklessly to interfere with or misuse anything required by law to protect the health, safety or welfare of others. The HSC guide, Managing Health and Safety in Schools, contains further detailed advice on these aspects.

A working environment in which all concerned co-operate to create good conditions will normally be a safer and happier place than one where they do not. Pupils should be encouraged to develop confidence and a sense of responsibility for themselves and others. They must learn to understand that their actions directly affect other people's safety, and be encouraged to look for, and react to, potential hazards. Pupils should be trained to work sensibly and safely, and to acquire positive attitudes towards safe practice. Teachers must give a clear lead by their own planning, precepts and personal example.

Heads of departments in secondary schools will often have certain safety functions delegated in connection with the legal requirements referred to in section 2. They and their staff should demonstrate a continuous commitment to health and safety requirements and set a good example for pupils to follow. It is important for pupils to recognise that everyone is involved and the responsibility is shared by all. By frequent reference to safety requirements and art department rules, a high standard of safety awareness can be attained and a working environment in which all concerned co-operate to create safe and harmonious conditions conducive to learning.

Safe working practices are dependent upon:

- commitment and a sound health and safety policy
- common sense, good management and organisation
- general awareness of requirements and shared responsibility
- properly planned and maintained accommodation
- appropriate techniques, use of tools and materials
- the use of adequate safety devices
- a knowledge and awareness of potential hazards.

3.1 Key Management Health and Safety Functions

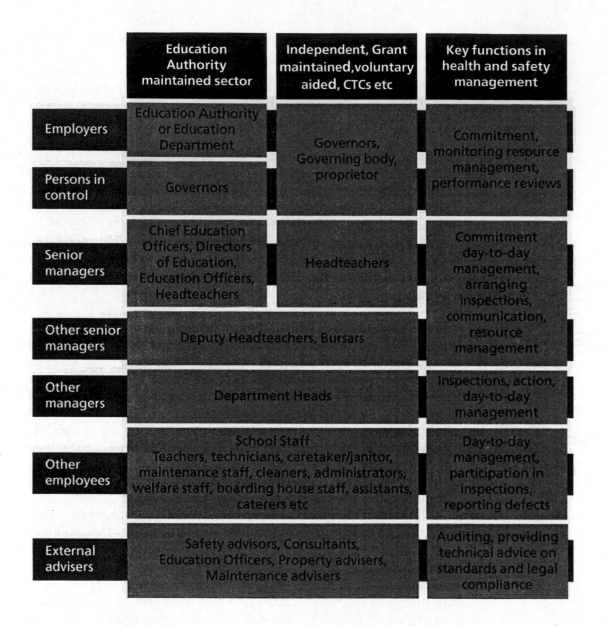

	Education Authority maintained sector	Independent, Grant maintained, voluntary aided, CTCs etc	Key functions in health and safety management
Employers	Education Authority or Education Department	Governors, Governing body, proprietor	Commitment, monitoring resource management, performance reviews
Persons in control	Governors		
Senior managers	Chief Education Officers, Directors of Education, Education Officers, Headteachers	Headteachers	Commitment day-to-day management, arranging inspections, communication, resource management
Other senior managers	Deputy Headteachers, Bursars		
Other managers	Department Heads		Inspections, action, day-to-day management
Other employees	School Staff Teachers, technicians, caretaker/janitor, maintenance staff, cleaners, administrators, welfare staff, boarding house staff, assistants, caterers etc		Day-to-day management, participation in inspections, reporting defects
External advisers	Safety advisors, Consultants, Education Officers, Property advisers, Maintenance advisers		Auditing, providing technical advice on standards and legal compliance

3.2 Special Educational Needs

In following advice offered in this publication, account should be taken of:

- the pupil's ability to understand instructions, follow them and understand any dangers involved
- the pupil's ability to communicate any difficulty or discomfort
- any physical disability which might affect the pupil's ability to perform a task safely
- any medical condition which may be adversely affected by exposure to equipment or materials.

It follows that particular care must be taken to ensure safe practice when tasks are undertaken by pupils with special educational needs. Attaining the right level of supervision is an important consideration. Children should be encouraged to achieve as much independence as is compatible with their disability. They should not be asked to perform tasks which are likely to be beyond their capabilities.

There are many disabilities which cannot be detected in the course of normal working, and some medical conditions which react adversely only in particular circumstances. It is important for teachers to know about the medical conditions of any pupils which may give rise to risk in certain activities.

Care should be taken to ensure that children are not put at risk because they have a limited understanding of safe practice.

4 Management and Organisation

4.1 School Management

Good management is the key to effective teaching and learning, and largely determines the ethos of a school. In schools where a high priority is given to sensible behaviour, concern for others and the orderly conduct of normal activities, safety is to some extent inherent. In practical activities this ethos forms the basis for safe working practices, but additional codes and constraints may be needed for particular activities. In general, the majority of materials, small tools and equipment used for art are perfectly safe, but there is an increasing range of materials and equipment which is potentially hazardous. Whilst much of the advice on specialised equipment and materials applies mainly to secondary schools, the requirements of National Curriculum Art has increased the range of work in many primary schools as well. Primary teachers who are using equipment and materials for the first time should refer to the appropriate sections in this booklet.

Well organised systematic procedures that contribute to both efficiency and safety should be established. Pupils should have a clear understanding of what they are expected to do and how to do it. Teachers should prepare materials and equipment thoroughly and know what constraints need to be exercised in their use.

4.2 Class management

Class management and the efficient use of available space are both important. There must be sufficient room for pupils to work without potentially dangerous physical contact, and to perform required tasks satisfactorily. It is also important to ensure that safe and easy access to materials and equipment is part of normal established procedures.

In general, it is important to establish a purposeful working environment in which there is a sense of order, concern for others and unhurried movement when performing technical operations.

4.3 Organisation

Organisation of both general classrooms and specialised studios will vary according to the range of art activities which can be undertaken. In primary classrooms where a variety of activities can take place simultaneously, much of the equipment and materials will probably be portable and little fixed equipment will be used. The likely hazards would mainly arise through the complexity of the different activities and the use of scissors, knives and similar equipment. In such circumstances it is particularly important to maintain proper levels of supervision. Good organisation, arrangement of working areas, access to materials and equipment, and careful supervision are the main ways of ensuring safe working conditions.

A multiplicity of activities may also take place in secondary school studios, mostly related to art. Such rooms will often accommodate a range of activities, from drawing and painting to claywork and printmaking. These are not necessarily compatible. Safe working practice depends upon the extent to which the art room is properly organised and the pupils are confident and competent to work in the variety of materials available. No pupil should be asked to attempt potentially hazardous tasks which are beyond their capabilities, and care should be taken to ensure that pupils do not use equipment for which they have not been trained.

Most secondary schools have some rooms dedicated to specialised activities such as ceramics and printmaking, and these require appropriate specific safety measures. Other sections of this booklet will deal with specialised activities in detail but the same principles of efficient organisation apply. In all cases adequate space is a pre-requisite of safe practice.

4.4 Untidiness

Poor organisation of storage and access systems for equipment and materials and work in progress may also create hazards. Clutter in circulation spaces and untidy, inaccessible and over-full storerooms present obstacles to safe movement and create a potential fire risk.

All these factors need to be taken into account in the planning and conduct of practical sessions. A regular monitoring system can help to ensure that account has been taken of any new hazards.

4.5 Maintenance

A regular, systematic maintenance programme for fabric, furniture, fittings, machinery, tools and other equipment can form an important part of the health and safety monitoring system. Items which require regular maintenance should if necessary be identified and listed in a schedule which is planned and checked each year, or more often if necessary. Some art departments in secondary schools may have technical assistance available, in which case the respective management responsibilities of the teacher and technician should be clearly understood. In the absence of a technician it is the responsibility of the head of department or subject teacher initially to ensure that adequate maintenance is provided and that equipment which requires regular maintenance is drawn to the attention of senior management for appropriate action.

Regular inspection and checks on items such as electrical apparatus, plugs, wires, sinks and drains are precautions which should be part of the management and organisation systems of any school or department. The Electricity at Work Regulations (1989) require periodic checks to be carried out by a competent person on all electrical apparatus. Such checks should ensure that equipment is maintained in an efficient working condition to prevent risk of injury (see DFE Building Bulletin 76, Maintenance of Electrical Services 1992). A free leaflet, Maintaining portable electrical equipment in offices and other low-risk areas, is also available from the HSE (see section 8).

4.6   Group Sizes

The Education (School Premises) Regulations (1981) do not specify maximum pupil numbers in relation to individual teaching spaces. However, there is an obvious relationship between the degree of hazard and the size of the teaching group in certain activities. For example, in specialised studios, such as ceramics, the space may have been planned with maximum numbers of around 20 pupils in mind, but in large art rooms there is usually sufficient room for up to 30 pupils, depending on the activity. Full class sizes of around 30 pupils might, however, place constraints on the range of activities which can safely be accommodated.

The size of practical groups and pupil-teacher ratios should take account of the assessment of potential hazards and appropriate safety regulations. Local authorities and other employers may issue guidelines on staffing ratios for practical subjects. This does not remove the direct management responsibility from the teaching staff, who must take account of the age, ability, aptitude and special educational needs of the pupils in relation to the accommodation, equipment and activities.

4.7   Fire Precautions

Day-to-day maintenance of the building and equipment to ensure fire safety are the ultimate responsibility of management. But all staff and pupils must be thoroughly familiar with the fire drill and understand the use of fire extinguishers, fire blankets and sand pails. These appliances should be kept inside the workroom as near to the door as possible, but remote from the area of the room where the fire risk is greatest. Rags, cotton waste, polyurethane foam and similar materials are a potential danger and should not be allowed to accumulate or be stored near naked flames or very hot objects. Aerosol containers should not be stored near naked flames or very hot objects, nor should they be punctured, even when empty. Some local authorities issue guidance to schools about the storage of flammable materials, including some adhesives, many solvents, finishes and other fluids, and cylinder gases. These should be followed at all times. Storage for bulk stocks differs from that necessary for smaller quantities in daily use.

Activities within practical areas, or displays of work (for example, on open days), should never obstruct access to fire escape routes or emergency exits.

4.8   First aid in the classroom

The Department has recommended that employers base their assessment of the appropriate number of qualified first aiders on the potential risks to pupils. Amongst the factors which should be considered are the age range and activities of the children, the nature of potential hazards and the layout of the building. It can be useful for all art and design staff to have at least a basic knowledge of first aid so they can offer assistance in the case of accidents. If the art department is in a separate block it would be particularly useful for at least one of the staff to hold a valid first aid certificate.

Pupils and all staff should be clear about the safety rules associated with the art department and the appropriate steps to take in any emergency, including evacuation procedures. All pupils should be told what to do if they have an accident, and this advice should be repeated regularly. First aid kits must be provided in every school and kept in easily accessible places known to teachers and pupils. There should be at least one kit in the art department of a secondary school, and where there are several specialist studios, workshops or classrooms each room should have one.

The names of the nearest first aiders should be displayed on all school notice boards. They should also be listed on each first aid box, together with instructions for dealing with burns, electrical shock and asphyxiation. The location of telephones, and the numbers to ring in case of emergency, should also be displayed.

The first aid box should be clearly labelled and made of suitable material designed to protect the contents from damp and dust. The contents should be simple, usable by any member of staff, and appropriate to the needs of the school. A kit should include:

- a card with general first aid guidance
- a supply of individually-wrapped sterile adhesive dressings appropriate to the work undertaken
- sterile eye pads with attachments
- triangular bandages (preferably sterile, but if not, sterile covering appropriate for serious wounds should also be included)
- a selection of sterile wound dressings, which should include medium-sized sterile unmedicated dressings (approximately 10cm x 8cm - standard dressings nos 8 and 13 BPC)
- large sterile unmedicated dressings (approximately 13cm x 9cm -standard dressings nos 9 and 14 BPC and the Ambulance dressing no 1)
- extra-large sterile unmedicated dressings (approximately 28cm x 17.6cm - Ambulance dressing no 3)
- safety pins.

The use of antiseptics is not necessary for the first aid treatment of wounds. Your school medical officer can advise on any additional items. The contents should be regularly checked to ensure that the necessary stocks are maintained. If there is a possibility that clothing might have to be cut away, blunt-ended stainless steel scissors (minimum length 12.7cm) should be stored in an appropriate place.

Whenever possible mains tap water should be used for eye irrigation - if this is not readily available sterile water or normal saline solution (0.9 per cent) in sterile packs should be provided. Eyebaths, cups and refillable containers should not be used for eye irrigation.

Disposable plastic gloves and bags for soiled or used dressings should also be provided near the first aid equipment and checked regularly to ensure that the stock is maintained and in good condition. Local authorities should be contacted for advice concerning disposal.

All accidents, however minor, should be recorded (see section 2.2.12 and 2.3 covering legal requirements, and details of further guidance in section 8).

4.9 First Aid and HIV

Qualified first aiders will be aware of the precautions which must be taken to avoid possible infection by the HIV virus, but it is essential that anyone administering aid to an injured person should also know what to do. There are standard precautions which reduce the risk of transmitting other infections, including hepatitis, and they are equally effective against HIV.

Exposed cuts and abrasions should always be covered up before giving treatment to an injured person and hands should be washed before and after applying dressings.

Whenever blood or other body fluids have to be mopped up, disposable plastic gloves and an apron should be worn; these items should then be placed in plastic bags and disposed of safely, preferably by burning. Clothing may be cleaned in an ordinary washing machine using the hot cycle.

The HIV virus is killed by household bleach and the area in which any spills have occurred should be disinfected using one part of bleach to ten parts of water; caution should be exercised as bleach is corrosive and can be harmful to the skin.

If direct contact with another person's blood or other body fluids occurs the area should be washed as soon as possible with ordinary soap and water. Clean cold water should be used if the lips, mouth, tongue, eyes or broken skin are affected, and medical advice should be sought.

Mouthpieces are available for first aiders giving mouth-to-mouth resuscitation, but they must only be used by properly trained persons. Mouth-to-mouth resuscitation should never be withheld in an emergency because a mouthpiece is not available. No case of infection has been reported from any part of the world as a result of giving mouth-to-mouth resuscitation.

For further information see the booklet AIDS and Employment, published by the Department of Employment and the HSE.

4.10 Chemicals

All corrosive and toxic chemicals, including many cleaning fluids, adhesives, dyes and inks, must be kept in secure stores under lock and key; quantities in use should be restricted to the minimum necessary. Teachers should be aware of the dangers, including those arising from accidental or intentional inhaling (glue-sniffing). Procedures for disposal and action in the event of an accident must be clearly set out in areas where chemicals are stored or used. It is advisable to arrange for some chemicals to be stored with bulk stock in other departments rather than duplicating storage in each.

Staff should bear in mind the requirements of the COSHH regulations and ensure that the appropriate precautions are put into practice. Care should be taken in selecting appropriate warning notices and safety signs to achieve maximum impact.

4.11 Electricity and Gas

Portable power tools and a wide range of gas, electrical and mechanical appliances are increasingly used in schools. The potential dangers, the special safety requirements and the importance of proper electrical and gas connections must be known and understood. Any faulty equipment should be withdrawn from use until it is repaired. Electrical apparatus should be switched off after use and plugs removed from sockets. Main switches and valves should be turned off every night as a safety precaution and to maintain their efficient working order. Whenever the electricity or gas supply is cut off for any reason, all switches controlling any appliances should be put in the off positions. Ideally, all electrical outlets should incorporate warning lights and, where appropriate, safety signs.

A notice should be displayed giving information on first aid treatment for electric shock.

Any gas appliances which have not been properly installed or serviced may produce dangerous carbon monoxide fumes. Gas appliances should be serviced regularly by a competent person who is trained in accordance with HSE standards and is familiar with the requirements. An outline of the Gas Safety (Installation and Use) Regulations (1994) is given in the HSE leaflet Gas Appliances - Keep them serviced - Keep them safe (1994) and the British Gas guidance notes for educational establishments (see sections 5.2.5, 5.2.6 and 8).

4.12 Pace-Makers and Artificial Organs

An increasing number of disabled pupils and adults are now helped to lead normal lives by developments in microelectronics, but internal and external pace-makers and other artificial organs may suffer interference from some electrical equipment. In general people with implants will be able to use domestic electrical equipment, but it may be appropriate for their medical consultant to be approached for detailed advice in cases where high voltage equipment is to be used.

4.13 Protective Clothing

Risk assessments should be carried out to identify the need for personal protective equipment. Apart from overalls, the need for face shields, goggles, gloves and other special items must be carefully considered. Employers should have regard to the PPE Regulations (see section 2.2.5) when considering standards to be applied to pupils.

Good safety awareness includes the habit of wearing and caring for protective clothing and equipment. Sound organisation and appropriate care and storage should be taken into consideration. Equipment, such as goggles, shared by pupils must be cleaned before and after use to prevent the spread of infection.

Approved goggles or industrial spectacles must be worn whenever there may be a risk of dust, sparks, chemical splashes or other flying particles affecting the eyes. British Standard 2092 (1987) on eye protectors gives further comprehensive guidance (see section 8). Optical spectacles alone do not give adequate eye protection, and present an additional hazard unless they are shatter-proof. Visors or special goggles that fit over spectacles are necessary. Protective screens which offer eye protection are sometimes fitted to a machine. Frequent attention is needed to ensure that such protective devices do not impede vision. They must be renewed immediately recleaning becomes ineffective.

Masks or respirators must be worn in certain conditions - for instance, whenever non-soluble or toxic dusts and fumes are present, when pupils are abrading or machining plastic materials including expanded polystyrene, working continuously on a polishing machine, or spraying paint or chemicals. Masks or respirators should only be used when other methods of extraction are impracticable.

Spot checks are recommended to ensure that protective equipment is being worn when necessary. Faulty protective equipment must not be used. Defects should be reported immediately and equipment replaced if necessary.

4.14   Outside Visits and Work Away From School

In addition to work experience, there is an increasing emphasis on work which takes place outside the school (for example, visits to exhibitions, galleries, museums, art, craft and design studios, factories and other places of interest). This experience is a valuable part of education, but the possible hazards should be carefully considered. Teachers should ensure they are fully aware of the potential hazards in any activity proposed for pupils and that adequate safety precautions are in place. To this end, schools may consider making a prior visit to the intended place of study to assess potential risks. The employers' guidelines for visits should be followed and consideration should be given to the appropriate pupil-teacher ratio. The teacher is in loco parentis; he or she must take all reasonable care and brief pupils accordingly. In certain circumstances additional insurance cover might be advisable.

Work experience, work simulations, community service and conservation activities may require special arrangements to ensure the safety of participants and to give protection to others. A designer, maker or provider of materials or components has a responsibility to ensure as far as possible that recipients and users will be aware of any possible hazards. Pupils engaged in work experience schemes are bound by the legislation applicable to employees of a similar age.

Further advice and guidance is contained in the teachers' pack, Guidance on

Work Experience and Guidance for Work Placement Organisers, produced by HSE and issued to all schools in autumn 1994.

4.15 Cleaning

The Workplace (Health, Safety and Welfare) Regulations (1992) and Approved Code of Practice have significant implications for the cleaning of rooms where art activities take place. Risk assessments must be made and due regard taken of the COSHH Regulations concerning cleaning materials. Cleaning staff must be made aware of safety requirements.

In contrast to the organisation of cleaning services which are part of whole-school management, the daily routines which should apply to classrooms and studios are largely the responsibility of the teacher in charge. Common sense is again the best guide. Clean working conditions are part of the general environment needed for good teaching and learning.

Pupils should be taught that cleaning up, care of tools and equipment, and respect for materials are an essential part of safe and efficient practice in art, crafts and design activities. Pupils should as far as possible be encouraged to assume responsibility for clearing their own work space. The aim should be to reach a stage where they do it automatically as soon as they complete their work.

Clay and materials such as plaster create particular problems. Unless the cleaning is done thoroughly, residues will accumulate and clay dust will eventually become a health hazard. A good system is to ensure that work surfaces are wiped down by pupils thoroughly after use or, in general teaching rooms, that the surfaces are properly covered with newspaper or other disposable material.

Dry sweeping of floors in ceramics studios should be avoided. In rooms where clay has been used, it is recommended that floors should be washed or damp-cleaned and vacuumed using an approved industrial wet/dry vacuum cleaner. Any clay dropped on the floor should be removed as soon as possible and the floor checked at the end of each session.

All glaze and slip buckets should be wiped down after use and lids washed. Everything used during a lesson should be washed at the end of the session, including tools, cloths, stools, wedging slabs, wheels and so on.

5 Accommodation

The preceding sections have covered many significant safety factors in the management and organisation of accommodation, whether specialised or not. The following sections cover physical requirements, such as design and layout of art rooms, storage areas, fixed equipment, fixtures and fittings, services, emergency apparatus, floors and furnishing, and deal with spaces dedicated to specialised use.

5.1 Design and Layout of Art Rooms

When new accommodation is being planned, it is sensible to get specialised advice on the layout and specification of furniture and equipment. This can normally be obtained from local authority advisers or manufacturers of specialised equipment. The positioning of fixed machinery and furniture will have to take account of the required circulation space. The organisation of work spaces for disabled people has implications for access, furniture and equipment.

Maintenance of equipment and devices - including floors - requires careful management of studios, workshops and storage areas to ensure adequate and safe access free from obstruction.

The question of appropriate group sizes may need to be considered. The numbers of pupils using accommodation at any one time, taking into account the nature of the activity and the degree of supervision required, should be appropriate to the design, layout and organisation of accommodation (see section 4.6).

5.2 Services

The statutory requirements and associated advice on the provision of heating, lighting and ventilation is contained in Building Bulletin 76, Maintenance of Electrical Services (HMSO, 1992), Building Bulletin 70, Maintenance of Mechanical Services, (HMSO, 1990) and DFE Design Note 17, Guidelines for Environmental Design and Fuel Consumption in Educational Buildings.

5.2.1 Lighting

Appropriate lighting to the required standards should be provided; a good spread of light, both natural and artificial, is of prime importance. Practical activities, particularly those requiring sharp tools, will often need supplementary lighting. Adjustable spotlights can be helpful, but avoid glare or excessive contrasts of light and shade. Whilst good natural lighting is desirable for machine operations, care should be taken to ensure that direct sunlight does not make flames and cutting surfaces invisible. Where electric lighting is used it is important to choose lamps with excellent colour rendering. Subdued lighting should be provided for forging, welding and brazing (British Standard BS4163).

5.2.2 Heating

The heating system should take into account the nature of the activity and ensure that there is an even, controlled temperature throughout the work space. Poor heating can be hazardous, either by creating conditions in which fingers are insufficiently flexible to control tools or by inducing drowsiness through excessive temperatures, lack of ventilation or poor air circulation.

Fan-assisted heating systems in ceramics studios, or rooms where clay is used frequently, create a potential hazard, particularly from ceramic micro-dust circulated by blown air. Where new accommodation is planned, such heating systems should not normally be installed. In existing accommodation with fan-assisted heating, risk can be substantially reduced by thorough cleaning each time clay is used and ensuring filters are fitted to fan converters and are cleaned regularly.

5.2.3 Ventilation

Normal ventilation requirements should apply in general art and design rooms, but ceramics studios, photography darkrooms and areas where there is an increased risk from spraying, fixing or cleaning with solvents have specific requirements above normal levels. It is, however, difficult for teachers to assess ventilation needs and provide what is often described vaguely as 'adequate ventilation'. Expert advice should always be sought about ventilation to kiln rooms, darkrooms and areas for spraying. A sound general principle is to reduce the need for ventilation by substituting, if possible, processes which do not require it.

In kiln rooms, extract ventilation applied by means of a suitable hood and fan system should be installed to provide a sufficient number of air changes each hour for the size of the room. Expert advice should be sought on this.

In schools where kilns are installed in classrooms or studios, teachers should ensure that there is adequate fresh air circulation. Should this prove to be difficult to achieve, or the kiln is likely to be used frequently when classes are in progress, mechanical ventilation may be necessary and expert advice should be obtained. Only normal biscuit and glaze firings should be made in kilns sited in working areas.

A suitable extract ventilation system must be installed in all darkrooms. It should be light-proof and provide an adequate number of air changes per hour for the size of room. Expert advice should again be sought.

All spray booths must have an air extraction system connected to the outside. If this is not possible, spray booths should not be installed.

Solvents of various kinds, fixatives and other aerosols, glues and adhesives should be used by an open window, or in mechanically-ventilated conditions if the activity is regular or prolonged. It is always sensible to limit the number of users at any one time, the length of continuous sessions, and the area of the room in which such processes are used.

5.2.4 Water supply and drainage

Taps and sinks should be sited conveniently to allow easy access and prevent crowding at a single point in an art room. They should be distanced from electrical supplies and apparatus. Draining boards should be kept clear for drainage purposes and not used for storage. Wet floors present a high safety risk, so leaks and spillages should be attended to immediately. Cleanliness is essential to safety and good health. Any blocked or dirty sinks may present a serious health risk.

Bottle traps should be fitted to sinks which are used for clay and other materials which leave sediments. They must be emptied and cleaned regularly. It is important to ensure that drainage is efficient and the drains do not get blocked by plaster, clay and other deposits. Plaster should not be poured down the sink, as it will block the drains. It should be allowed to dry and then disposed of as solid waste. On no account must flammable substances be put down drains.

5.2.5 Electrical Equipment

Detailed advice on electrical safety can be obtained from DFE Building Bulletin 76, Maintenance of Electrical Services (1992), the Electricity at Work Regulations (1989), which make periodic maintenance of electrical equipment a statutory requirement, and HSE Guidance Note GS23, Electrical Safety in Schools. However, when planning new or modifying existing electrical services some important general principles must be observed.

All power outlets must be placed in accessible positions away from water supplies and drainage. They should not be placed where leads will have to cross circulation routes, and should be at a reasonable height above the floor. There should be sufficient outlets to support the range of equipment normally used without resorting to unnecessary multi-socket adaptors.

Isolators for all circuits should be placed in readily accessible positions with local isolators of the non-self-resetting type fitted to each fixed machine. The conversion of hand-operated machines to power operation, such as printing presses, should never be undertaken without appropriate advice being sought beforehand, and without having the modifications checked by a suitably qualified person before they are used.

Electrically-fired kiln doors should be fitted with an approved system to ensure that the mains electricity supply is isolated before the door is opened. This may either be a fail-safe positively operated switch (used on some small kilns) or an interlock system, trapped key or similar device. Bright warning lights to indicate that the mains supply is on should be mounted in duplicate in a prominent part of the studio. Kiln loading by pupils must be closely supervised.

Automatic electronically-controlled firing mechanisms are now readily available and relatively inexpensive, and should be fitted to kilns in preference to hand-operated systems, which are vulnerable to human error.

Electrically-fired kilns sited in a working area should be protected by a cage and have an interlock system or padlock fitted to the door to prevent opening during firing.

In the case of portable electric power tools, a sensitive residual current device (often referred to as an earth leakage current-breaker unit) of the current balance type should be used as back-up protection when any appliance is used at mains voltage. Whenever possible, a low-voltage electricity supply should be installed.

All exposed, non-current-carrying metal parts of both fixed and portable equipment must be effectively earthed unless the equipment is double-insulated. Two concentric squares marked on the rating plate of the equipment indicates that it is double-insulated.

Ratings of fuses should be related to the type of equipment. Switches or fuses should always break the live lead, which must be coloured red or brown. New standard PVC-sheathed flexible cable should be used and the terminal wiring and polarity checked. Wiring on old or foreign equipment not conforming to European standards should be changed. All leads deteriorate with use, so regular checks must be made in accordance with the requirements of the Electricity at Work Regulations (1989) (see section 4.5).

Pilot lights should be installed wherever possible and checked regularly.

5.2.6 Gas Supplies and Gas-Burning Appliances

Gas supply points should be positioned so that they are easily accessible and free from obstruction. Work surfaces for gas appliances, such as gas rings for wax melting, should be properly designed for stability and ease of use. Care should be taken to position the appliances so that pupils cannot accidently lean over them when working.

All mains gas supplies to equipment such as brazing torches should be controlled in each work area by a well-positioned emergency master valve. This should be turned off every night to prevent hazards and accidents, and to ensure that it is kept in effective working order. Main control taps or valves should be clearly labelled.

Gas kilns should not be used in schools unless the staff have had specialist training in firing procedures. All members of staff firing gas kilns should be aware of the 'lock-out' procedure and of how to prevent the risk of explosion by blow-back during lighting. A canopy to direct heat and fumes away from the kiln directly to the outside atmosphere is necessary. Many local authorities have stringent regulations governing installation.

An increasing number of kilns are fuelled by bottled gas. If their use is approved by employers, the manufacturer's instructions for the safe siting and operation of such kilns should be strictly observed. Propane gas cylinders must be stored in the regulation conditions (see the HSE guide The keeping of liquid petroleum gases in cylinders and similar containers).

The British Gas publication IM/25, Guidance Note on Gas Safety in Educational Establishments, provides further useful information.

5.2.7 Storage

Storerooms should be sufficiently large to meet the needs of the areas they serve and take account of the range and type of activities. For example, studios undertaking a lot of three-dimensional work will require storage for bulky materials and work in progress. An area of 0.4m2 to 0.5m2 for each pupil place may be used as a guide. Failure to provide sufficient storage space can result in an accumulation of materials in working areas.

Racks and storage units should be positioned for ease of access and should not reduce or obstruct circulation space. High-level storage units should not be used for heavy equipment or materials, and safe means of access should be provided.

Storage spaces should be equipped with appropriate systems for keeping stock and work in progress in a tidy, accessible manner. Untidy, cluttered or overfull storerooms constitute fire hazards and other dangers. Adequate lighting and ventilation should be installed. Appropriate storage for personal protective equipment and pupils' outdoor clothing should be provided.

In ceramics areas, separate storage is required for work awaiting firing (the kiln room may be suitable for this), damp storage for clay and work in progress, and for bulk materials, slips and glazes. Combustible materials should not be stored in the kiln room.

Compressed gases such as propane, acetylene and LPG (liquefied petroleum gases) are subject to stringent storage regulations which must be observed. It is unlikely that an art department will have a need for separate bulk storage facilities and it is recommended that all such gases are kept in a properly designed school store.

Flammable liquids and highly flammable liquids (subject to the Highly Flammable Liquids and Liquefied Petroleum Gases Regulations, 1972) require special, suitably marked, lockable metal storage bins or cupboards which are designed and approved for the purpose. Up to 50 litres may be kept in a workroom if properly stored, but it is advisable to reduce the stored quantity to the lowest operational levels.

Petroleum spirit and mixtures are subject to the Petroleum (Consolidation) Act (1928). Less than three gallons of petroleum spirit may be kept with other flammable liquids in a flammable liquids cabinet. Quantities above this level require a petroleum storage licence obtainable from the local fire authority, which carries stringent conditions.

Very small quantities of flammable liquids (closed containers holding not more than 500cc) do not require special storage arrangements, but naturally still require careful thought as to where they are put.

Main stocks of acids and other corrosive substances should be kept in a main school store provided with a low-sited, ventilated and lockable cupboard, lined with acid-resistant material such as ceramic tiles, lead, stainless steel or stone. Only limited supplies of concentrated acid should be kept in the studio, in a cupboard which is strong, stable and properly locked. Acid should be kept in standard acid bottles.

6 Machines, Equipment, Tools and Processes

This section covers siting, safety guards and devices, safe working practices.

The location of all fixed machinery and equipment must meet the requirements of all safety regulations and expert advice should be sought before fixing positions.

British Standard BS 4163 (1984), Code of Practice for Health and Safety in Workshops of Schools and Similar Establishments states that where electrical equipment is installed, it should be possible to isolate all electrical circuits that supply fixed equipment and socket outlets by means of a single switch disconnecter, complying with British Standard European Norm BS EN 60947 specification for low switch gear and control gear. Switches, disconnecters, switch disconnecters and fuse combinations units. (see HSC Memorandum of Guidance on the Electricity at Work Regulations (1989)).

All machinery must be to a standard to meet statutory regulations, and be subject to regular, systematic maintenance.

6.1 Ceramics Machinery, Equipment and Working Methods

6.1.1 Pugmills

Some form of emergency switch disconnecter is essential. Such machines, including blungers, should only be used by authorised staff or strictly supervised by responsible persons. Pugmills should be fitted with a throat guard and clay should not be fed into the machine with this guard removed. A hand lever feeding device should be fitted for use in schools. On no account must the machine be run with the barrel open, outlet removed or drive guards removed.

It is recommended that a working area of at least one metre around the machine should be kept clear for operational purposes.

6.1.2 Blungers

These require similar precautions to pugmills. Hands should never be placed in the blunger tub or tank when the unit is working.

6.1.3 Potmills

An open roller drive rotates the pot, and although it does not rotate at high speed there is a risk that hands could be trapped by the motion.

6.1.4 Pottery Wheels

Electric and kick wheels should be guarded where moving parts create hazards. Manufacturers' guards should be securely in place whilst the machine is in use. There should be adequate space surrounding the wheel to operate in safety. Electric wheels must be properly earthed and sealed-unit waterproof switches should be fitted.

6.1.5   **Jiggers/Batting Machines**

Similar precautions should be taken as for pottery wheels.

6.1.6   **Lathes**

Belt-driven lathes should be well guarded. On no account should the ratios be changed without the lathe being isolated from the power source. Goggles should be worn, hair tied back if necessary and appropriate protective clothing worn. Loose material should not be brushed away from the lathe until it is turned off.

6.1.7   **Compressors**

Oil levels should be checked regularly, together with air filters and blow-off valves. Compressed air can penetrate the skin and cause serious damage if put in any of the body's orifices. Regular inspection of air receivers by a competent person is required for the purposes of insurance (Pressure Systems and Transportable Gas Containers Regulations, 1989).

6.1.8   **Spray Booths**

Booths should preferably be of the water-backed variety, but in exhaust booths the exhaust tubes should be checked for leakage and filters regularly cleaned. On no account should booths that are not vented to the exterior be installed.

6.1.9   **Bench-Mounted Off-Hand Grinders**

Grinders used for forming and sharpening tools and other equipment must be fitted with guards and appropriate goggles worn. Work rests should be adjusted to meet wheel wear. Nobody should use bench-mounted off-hand grinders unless they hold a certificate to prove that they are properly trained. Detailed information is contained in the Abrasive Wheels Regulations (1970).

6.1.10   **Kilns**

Kilns should normally be loaded by teachers or technicians, but it may be part of a pupil's course to learn kiln operations. Such work must always be carefully supervised and correct procedures for loading and unloading strictly observed. Care should be taken to avoid back strain through lifting heavy articles. Students should be instructed in the complete firing sequence and alerted to the hazards associated with improper removal of ventilation or inspection bungs during firing: blue or smoked glass should always be used to protect the eyes when inspecting temperature colour or flame action. The siting of kilns needs careful attention and adequate space should be allowed around and above them. Kilns situated in working areas should be caged and there must be adequate ventilation in the room. Detailed advice is available from the Institute of Materials.

Outdoor kilns should be adequately guarded and fuel stored away from heat sources. Care should be taken that smoke and fumes are not blown into surrounding buildings.

Ground flint should not be used for dusting kiln furniture or making batwash. If flint is required for other purposes it should be kept in either paste or slop form.

It is very important for the safe and efficient kiln operation that regular maintenance is carried out by qualified personnel. However, sensible 'first-line' maintenance, such as regular cleaning, is also essential.

More information on electric and gas kilns is given in sections 5.2.5 and 5.2.6 respectively.

6.1.11 Safe Working Methods

Safe working methods in ceramics are generally covered by the management and organisation advice in section 4. However, some working methods are specific to ceramics and need to be given particular attention.

Personal hygiene is important to reduce the risks from ceramics materials. Hands should be washed and nails scrubbed after using ceramics materials and chemicals. Some form of wet-work barrier cream may offer a degree of protection against possible allergic skin reactions. Protective overalls and aprons should be laundered regularly. Food should not be consumed or brought into working areas. Smoking should not be allowed. Cuts, burns and abrasions should be immediately and properly treated.

Fettling and the shaping of raw clay vessels by any other means should only be carried out when the clay is 'leather-hard'. On no account should it be done when the clay is dry.

Areas for working in clay and plaster should be kept separate. Plaster in clay can cause damaging explosions during the firing process.

On no account must lime plaster be used and the correct procedures for mixing and using plaster should be strictly observed.

Glass containers should not generally be used in art rooms to avoid the risk of broken glass.

Steps should be taken to ensure that clay storage bins cannot be mistaken for waste bins. Areas for clay reconstitution should be kept free from other materials.

Asbestos products should not be used to store or handle ceramic ware. Any existing equipment that is likely to contain visible or accessible asbestos, such as kilns, should be regularly monitored to ensure that the asbestos is not damaged (further advice can be obtained from your local HSE office).

Although less hazardous than asbestos, ceramic fibres (used as an alternative insulant to kilns) must also be treated with care - precautions must be taken to prevent physical contact and inhalation. Similar monitoring checks to those recommended for asbestos should be carried out.

6.2 Cutting Tools

6.2.1 Knives

Sharp knives and tools are needed for a variety of art work. For carving wood and other resistant materials it is important to use effective holding devices. For cutting or engraving wood, lino or hardboard for printmaking, the use of bench keys, or G-clamps for large blocks, will provide a more stable working surface. Tools which are properly sharp present less of a hazard than when bluntness causes the user to exert excessive pressure.

6.2.2 Shared Use

Where tools are used by a number of teachers, one person should have the main responsibility for their maintenance and storage. Care should be taken when lending tools to other people that they understand the potential hazards and return the tools promptly.

6.2.3 Care of Tools

It should be emphasised to pupils that the proper care and use of tools is an important part of their education.

6.2.4 Guillotines

Guillotines for cutting paper and card must be properly guarded at all times and only used by pupils under supervision. Bench shears for cutting metal should be locked when not in use.

6.3 Printing and Printmaking

6.3.1 Mechanical and Power-Driven Machines

All such machinery and equipment used in printmaking and printing should meet the statutory standards and regulations governing their use. Regular maintenance is essential. Presses should be adequately guarded and guards regularly checked for efficiency. There must be sufficient surrounding space for their safe operation. Hand-operated machines, such as etching presses, should have a means of preventing their use out of idle curiosity or deliberate tampering.

6.3.2 Screen Printing

Screen printing is reasonably risk-free, except for the use of oil-based inks and solvents. It is becoming increasingly difficult to meet the stringent standards set by the COSHH regulations on the use of solvent-based inks and processes, and the simple solution is to use toxic-free water-based inks instead. Some new products specifically designed to meet the needs and consisting of a mixture of acrylic paint and a screen-printing paste are excellent and generally risk-free.

There are important precautions to observe when using ultra-violet light boxes for exposing treated screens. Manufacturer's instructions and other regulations must be strictly observed.

6.3.3 Etching

Etching and other acid-based activities are subject to stringent regulations in the use of materials and conduct of operational processes. **Acid etching and polishing with hydrofluoric acid is a particularly hazardous operation and should not be carried out in schools.**

Acid solutions for etching must always be made up by the teacher or technician. The use of concentrated acid or a mixture of sulphuric and nitric acid as mordants for etching increases the potential dangers. **Acid must always be added to water when mixing solutions. Adding the water to the acid is extremely dangerous. Protective clothing should be worn.**

The acid bath should be located in a ventilated cupboard or have a lid, either of which should be locked when not in use.

Any spillage of acids should be carefully and quickly dealt with by neutralising with sodium carbonate powder before wiping up with a cloth or paper, which should be disposed of in such a way as not to cause further damage.

Provision of facilities for immediate eye irrigation or washing affected parts of the body with water is **essential** to minimise the danger of acid burns. Clean water from a plastic bottle, delivered as an upward jet, gives effective eye irrigation but acid burns to the eyes should be referred to the local eye clinic for further treatment immediately.

Storage of acids should be in accordance with the appropriate regulations (see section 5.2.7 for further details).

6.4 Textiles

6.4.1 Working with Dyes

General safety precautions are normally sufficient for work with textiles, but there are potential hazards in the use of some dyes, mordants and other chemicals (see section 7.9). Some dyes are water or oil emulsions and have to be fixed by placing the fabric in a warm oven. Unless the fabric is thoroughly dry, vapour from these dyes can ignite. Care should be taken to ensure that dyes are stored in a cool place. When mixing dye powder, it is sensible to mix a whole packet at a time. Preventing inhalation of dye powder by wearing masks, opening the packet under water or using a glove box is also sensible. Protective gloves should be worn.

6.4.2 Storage, Preparation and Handling of Dyes

The storage, preparation and handling of dyes, acids and solvents should always be in strict accordance with manufacturers' instructions and legal requirements (see sections 6.3.2 and 6.3.3, section 5.2.7 on storage, and section 7 under Materials).

6.4.3 Acetic Acid and Solvents

The use of concentrated acetic acid can be avoided by using vinegar instead. Solvents such as methylated spirits carry a fire risk and can be dangerous, especially to the eyes and if swallowed. Dyes requiring boiling water can be hazardous because of the risk of scalding - these should be used only in suitable working conditions.

6.4.4 Hot Wax

The use of hot wax for various processes can be a serious fire hazard. It should always be heated slowly in a specially designed pan suspended over a larger one partially filled with water. Care should be taken to prevent water getting into the hot wax container. The working surface should be firm and free from obstructions and the pan must be accessible without the user having to lean across other heating devices.

6.4.5 Mercury Vapour Lamps

Care should be taken to ensure that all proper precautions are taken when using ultra-violet and mercury vapour lamps for exposing screens. It is essential that appropriate eye protection is worn.

6.5 Photography

6.5.1 Darkrooms

In a properly organised and well-designed darkroom there should be few hazards. The greatest dangers arise from the proximity of electricity to water, lack of adequate ventilation and handling chemicals. (For information on ventilation and electrical equipment see sections 5.2.3 and 5.2.5; for chemicals see section 7.)

6.5.2 Developers

Developers employed in the processing of colour photographs (and to a lesser extent those used in processing black and white emulsions) may cause allergic reactions when brought into contact with the skin. Warnings to this effect, and recommendations for the avoidance of dermatitis, are contained in the manufacturers' instructions for the use of chemicals. Suitable rubber gloves should be made available.

6.5.3 The Processing Room

The processing room should be provided with a 'wet' area for all dish and tank processes, and a separate 'dry' bench for printing, enlarging and handling dry photo-sensitive materials.

Thermometers should not be used as stirring rods. Apart from the danger of broken glass, mercury and the vapour emitted is poisonous. Care should be taken in dealing with any breakages. When replacing this equipment spirit thermometers should be considered.

The 'wet' processing area should be constructed of chemical-proof material and be provided with a means of washing down all chemically contaminated surfaces after use. Hand rinsing and drying facilities should be provided, and care should be taken to dry hands thoroughly before touching electrical equipment.

Electrical fittings and sockets should be sited away from the 'wet' area and all electrical apparatus should be properly earthed. Pull-cord type switches are preferable to surface switches in darkrooms.

6.6 Computers and VDUs

The risks associated with the occasional use of computers in art and design education are thought to be very low. Concerns are being expressed, however, in relation to very low-frequency radiation, eye disorders and posture-related stresses. Teachers need to be aware that some photosensitive pupils may have an attack of epilepsy triggered by use of the VDU. Such cases are rare. But as the use of VDUs increases it is sensible to take simple precautions.

The image on the display screen should be clear and stable. Adequate, but not excessive, illumination should be provided, and harsh contrasts in background lighting should be avoided to prevent glare and distracting reflections.

Posture is important. Seating should be comfortable and adjustable. There should be sufficient space to allow postural changes. Back strain should be avoided by ensuring adequate support and not allowing pupils to sit for long periods without a break.

The work surface should allow a flexible arrangement of equipment, stability, low reflection and adequate space for hand support. There should be adequate work space around the unit. Cables and connections should be kept clear of possible interference, checked regularly and placed so that accidental contact is avoided. The work surface should be non-reflective in line with the Health and Safety (Display Screen Equipment) Regulations (see section 2.2.7).

The operator should sit at a reasonable distance from the screen - one metre seems to be a minimum for most people.

7 Materials

This section deals with materials which are not usually associated with one specific activity. For example, sculpture or experimental three-dimensional work may involve a considerable range of materials which may be duplicated in different activities. The most obvious danger is in the unorthodox or 'creative' use of processes and materials which, in other circumstances, may be prescribed by 'named' activities such as modelling, welding, casting, and so on.

7.1 Working in Metals

When engaged in such processes as forge-work, soldering, casting, welding and acid pickling, teachers should make detailed reference to British Standard BS 4163. In all these processes it is essential that the teacher is properly trained and qualified.

7.1.1 Metal Casting

When metal casting involves the use of polystyrene - the 'lost polystyrene' method - exhaust ventilation is essential. Polystyrene should never be cut with ordinary knives heated by application to a direct heat source. Cutting polystyrene with a hot wire generates phenylethene fumes. The cutter should be constructed to operate at an even heat which is just sufficient to cut. It is safer to use a battery operated cutter than one powered by a low tension supply. Cutting should be carried out only in well-ventilated conditions, for example, near an open window. In casting with other materials which may have a residual water content it is essential that the material is completely dry before molten metal is introduced. If not the risk of serious explosion is high. **Metal casting should not be attempted unless the teacher is properly trained and qualified and the conditions are appropriate.**

7.1.2 Oxy-Fuel Welding

Oxy-fuel welding and flame cutting should carried out only under the direction of a fully qualified teacher who has successfully completed an approved course of training.

7.1.3 Electric Welding

Electric welding must not be undertaken in art rooms.

7.2 Working with Wood

Some hardwoods produce dust which may be a respiratory hazard, particularly when created by machines. There is a risk of dermatitis, other adverse reactions and injury from splinters. Dust extraction units should be provided for machines such as disc and belt sanders. Cutting, shaping and piercing wood by both hand and machine methods should be done only when the material is securely held by mechanical devices. The use of woodworking machines is strictly regulated and teachers must be properly qualified. For detailed advice, reference should be made to the HSE's free booklet Supervising Safety in Woodworking, the National Association of Advisers and Inspectors in Design and Technology's publication Safety Training Courses for Teachers and Technicians using School Workshops and BS 4163 Code of Practice (1984) Health and Safety in Workshops Schools and Similar Establishments (see section 8).

7.3 Working in plastics

7.3.1 Types of Plastics

The two main forms of plastics likely to be used in schools are thermo-plastics and thermo-setting plastics. Thermo-plastics are formed in a reversible process and can therefore be restored to their original form by the application of heat. They have the flammable hazardous properties of liquids rather than solids, and can also give off toxic fumes at elevated temperatures. Thermo-setting plastics do not have reversible properties and are made by mixing polyester and other polymer resins with appropriate catalysts. Most resins, accelerators and solvents come within the scope of the Highly Flammable Liquids and Liquefied Petroleum Gases Regulations (1972), which must be strictly observed. **The preparation of polyurethane foam and other plastics should only be undertaken in a fume cupboard.**

7.3.2 Uncured Polyester Resin

Uncured polyester resin releases phenylethene fumes. Provided that only small quantities are being used and the area is well ventilated the fumes may not be harmful, but the risk involved depends upon an individual's sensitivity and therefore needs to be individually assessed.

7.3.3 Glass Fibre

Some airborne fibre glass dust particles can cause lung damage and synthetic resins can be harmful to the skin.

7.4 Working with Glass

There are many hazards associated with working in glass, but very few schools are likely to use the material extensively.

7.4.1 Batch Mixing and Loading

In batch mixing and loading in which silicaceous and toxic dusts are likely to be created, a batch must always be mixed in a sealed container and all appropriate safety measures must be observed.

7.4.2 Hot Glass

When working with hot glass, eye protection, protective clothing, safety spectacles and other appropriate personal protection precautions must be used. Kilns are subject to the same regulations and safety procedures as for ceramics kilns.

7.4.3 Cutting, Grinding and Polishing

Precautions should include the use of personal protective clothing, eye shields and glasses. Grinding wheels must be run at the appropriate settings for 'trueness' and wheel speeds, and enough water should be used to ensure coolness and remove waste.

7.4.4 Lead

Handling lead can result in particles being trapped under finger nails or accidentally ingested. Hands should be thoroughly washed and finger nails scrubbed, and care taken to keep hands away from the mouth when working.

7.4.5 Acid Etching and Polishing

Etching and polishing with hydrofluoric acid must not be attempted in schools.

7.5 Working with Building and Insulation Blocks

The health hazards of the compounds used in the manufacture of building and insulation blocks should be investigated before being carved or abraded. Some may have a high silica and irritant content.

All heavy materials which could cause severe damage to feet and hands if insecure must be held firmly in a suitable vice or other mechanical device.

7.6 Ceramic Materials

Most of the advice on safe working practices is contained in section 6.1. However there are many potentially hazardous materials used in ceramics work and teachers need to ensure that the most dangerous are not used in schools. Detailed advice is available in the Institute of Materials' booklet Health and Safety in Ceramics (1991).

7.6.1 Lead

The use of raw lead compounds is forbidden in schools (DFE Administrative Memorandum 517). Glazes containing more than five per cent soluble lead should not be used at all in schools, and strict precautions should be taken with other glazes. However, the presence of heavy metal compounds such as lead or cadmium in glazes does not constitute a hazard providing they are correctly formulated, applied and fired.

7.6.2 Glazes Subject to Acid Attack

Glazes applied to pottery such as plates, mugs and dishes which may be used for food and drink must be carefully chosen, since some are subject to acid attack resulting in the release of lead, cadmium or other toxins. Copper should not be added to any glaze intended for food contact surfaces. Blending glazes or components should be avoided, as this can result in products with unknown acid durability. In such circumstances a metal release test should be carried out to determine whether the necessary safety standard has been achieved (see BS6748 (1986) specification for Limits of Metal Release from Ceramic Ware, Glassware, Glass Ceramic Ware and Vitreous Enamel Ware).

Information on the current lead and cadmium release limits can be obtained from local authority trading standards and consumer protection departments or British Ceramic Research Limited.

7.6.3 Dust from Dry Clay

Dust from dry clay and glazes constitutes the chief hazard in a ceramics studio. Good management and cleaning will reduce the hazards considerably (see section 4.15). Dry materials should be stored in sealed containers, and both wet and dry spillage should be cleaned up immediately.

7.6.4 Toxic Materials

There are many ceramic materials other than lead which are toxic, and teachers should ensure that information is supplied when they are bought and the suppliers' instructions are strictly observed. It is essential that all materials are properly labelled and stored, and that appropriate warnings are included in the labelling. One of the main reasons for insisting upon the regular and thorough washing of hands is to avoid toxic hazards.

7.6.5 Glazes in General

Eyes and skin should be protected when using glazes, and good washing facilities are essential. Food and drink should not be allowed in areas where glazes are being used. Glazes containing chromium are severe skin irritants. During glaze preparation dry materials should be added to water, not water added to the dry material, to minimise dust.

7.6.6 Firing

The reason for insisting upon adequate ventilation is that during firing various glaze materials break down. For example, Cornish stone releases fluorine and wood ash produces sulphur dioxide if not thoroughly washed; enamel media and lustres produce acrid fumes during the initial stages of firing; and noxious, sulphurous fumes are released by some fire clays during firing.

7.6.7 Over-Firing.

Glazes which are fired for too long or at too high a temperature can release volatile materials into the atmosphere. For example, lead becomes volatile at around 1180°C, so a low-solubility lead glaze would release lead-bearing fumes.

7.7 Paints

Most paints used in schools are perfectly safe, but some practices may create hazards.

7.7.1 Pigments

The use of dry pigments to make up paint can lead to inhaling dust. Personal protective equipment may be necessary. Some pigments may contain carcinogenic substances, such as arsenic and chrome.

7.7.2 Paint Spraying

The spraying of paint by airbrush, aerosol or on a larger scale with compressed air may produce a fine mist of pigment dust in the air, with solvent vapours which can then be inhaled. If large or regular amounts of spraying are done, a spray booth with exhaust or water-backed ventilation should be used. In any case, good ventilation is essential for all paint spraying.

7.7.3 Ingestion of Paints

The practice of licking or pointing a paint brush by mouth may result in the ingestion of toxic pigments.

7.8 Solvents

7.8.1 Volatile Substances

Solvents are generally highly volatile and toxic substances. They constitute the most common source of hazardous fumes in art and craft processes. Users of solvents or media containing solvents should find out exactly what they are and what they contain. This information is obtainable from the manufacturer or supplier.

7.8.2 Skin Irritants

Some solvents are primary skin irritants. Others may produce dermatitis and, by dissolving the natural grease of the skin, make it more vulnerable to damage by other substances.

7.8.3 Inhalation

Inhalation is the most common way in which toxic materials can enter the body. It is therefore very important that inhalation of solvent vapours is kept to a minimum. If work with solvents is carried out regularly, or on a large scale, appropriate means of ventilation must be installed.

7.8.4 Tetrachloromethane

Tetrachloromethane, although non-flammable, is highly toxic and should not be used.

7.8.5 Propanone

Propanone is one of the least toxic solvents, but it is highly flammable and should be used with extreme care.

7.8.6 Turpentine

Turpentine is neither highly toxic nor highly flammable, but it can be a primary skin irritant and possibly produce allergic reactions.

7.8.7 Aerosols

Aerosols present a considerable hazard, due to the presence of probably toxic and flammable solvents and other substances. They should be avoided if possible, but otherwise only used in a well-ventilated specialist area. They should never be used when other people are near.

7.9 Dyes

Careful selection and use is essential. Care should be taken to avoid accidental inhalation, ingestion or skin absorption.

7.9.1 Dye Powders

Dye powders are very fine, and therefore dangerous if inhaled. They should be mixed when wholly immersed in water or, if this is not possible, a dust mask or respirator should be worn. Heavy-duty rubber gloves should be worn to avoid skin contamination. Cooking utensils should not be used, as they may retain potentially hazardous amounts of chemicals. Personal protective clothing should be worn and there should be no eating, drinking or smoking in a dyeing area. Only soap and water should be used to remove splashes from the skin, as chemical substances such as bleach or potassium mangate (VII) might break down the dyes into hazardous substances.

7.9.2 Direct Dyes

Direct benzidine-type dyes are a component of all-purpose dyes. These may be toxic and care should be exercised.

7.9.3 Acid Dyes

These are used for silk and wool, and are probably the least hazardous.

7.9.4 Basic Dyes

These dyes, used for wool, silk and some synthetics, may cause allergic reactions.

7.9.5 'Procion' Dyes

These are also known as fibre-reactive or cold water dyes. Reactive dyes are extremely reactive chemical compounds and are capable of reacting with body tissue. The respiratory tract is particularly sensitive to reactive dyes and allergic responses may occur. Symptoms may seem like hay-fever or asthma, accompanied by swollen eyes.

7.9.6 Synthetic Mordant Dyes

These may be used in dyeing wool, and the most hazardous mordant salt is potassium dichromate. Other metal salts such as chromium cobalt, copper and so on may be both toxic and corrosive, and it is recommended that alum (potassium aluminium sulphate) salts of tin or iron be used instead.

7.9.7 Azoic Dyes

The constituent materials of these dyes, 'fast bases' (fast salts) and 'napthol', are highly reactive chemical compounds capable of causing dermatitis and other skin disorders.

7.10 Working with Scrap Materials

Scrap materials are often used in schools, particularly for three-dimensional work. They are a cheap means of extending the range of activities and encouraging creative adaptation. They also raise consciousness of ecological issues and recycling. There are, however, obvious hazards related to storage, manipulation and processing.

7.10.1 Handling, Shaping and Cutting

These processes, along with joining and dismantling, are all potentially hazardous and care should be taken to ensure that materials and objects are held securely and handled with care in an appropriate working environment.

7.10.2 Treating Surfaces

Treating surfaces which are already painted, dyed or covered with unknown materials should also be done carefully. Since little will be known about the composition of such surface materials, burning or the application of other chemicals can cause hazardous reactions.

7.10.3 Personal Hygiene

Hands should be thoroughly washed after working. Appropriate personal protective clothing should be worn and care taken to avoid inhalation or ingestion of unknown substances.

7.10.4 Storage

Storage of scrap materials should be considered as part of normal 'housekeeping', and regular clear-outs should be made.

7.11 Adhesives and Fixatives

7.11.1 Irritants

Some forms of adhesives, such as epoxy resins, can be irritants. Sensible precautions must be taken to avoid skin contact. If it is considered necessary to use contact adhesives that give off heavy, toxic or flammable vapours, good ventilation is essential. Aerosol-propelled fixatives and adhesives should only be used in controlled conditions with adequate ventilation (see section 5.2.3).

7.11.2 'Super Glues'

These cyanocyrlate-based adhesives, which can instantly bond body tissues, should not be used by children.

7.11.3 Petroleum-Based Adhesives

These must be properly stored (see sections 4.7 and 5.2.7).

7.11.4 Addictive Habits

Teachers should be aware of the addictive and dangerous habits that can arise from sniffing some adhesives and fixatives.

8 Further information

Management of Health and Safety

The Management of Health and Safety at Work Regulations (1992) SI 1992 No 2051, ISBN 0 11 025051 6, HMSO, price £2.30.

HSC *Managing Health and Safety in Schools* (1994), ISBN 0 7176 0770 4, price £5.00.

HSC *Management of Health and Safety at Work Approved Code of Practice* (1992), ISBN 0 71 760412 8, price £5.00.

HSC *The Responsibilities of School Governors for Health and Safety* (1992), ISBN 0 71 760436 5, price £3.50.

HSE leaflet 5 Steps to Risk Assessment (1994) free from HSE Books

DFE series *School Governors: A Guide to the Law* (1994) for:

County, Controlled and Special Agreement Schools
Aided Schools
Self-Governing (Grant-Maintained) Schools
Special Schools.

Copies of the separate editions are available from Westex, Department for Education, PO Box 2193, London E15 2EU.

First aid

Employment Department and HSE *AIDS and the Workplace: A guide for employers*, free booklets available from Cambertown, Unit 4, Commercial Road, Goldthorpe Industrial Estate, Goldthorpe, Rotherham, South Yorkshire S63 9BL, quoting reference PL893.

DFE *HIV and AIDS: A Guide for the Education Service* available free from Westex, Department for Education, PO Box 2193, London E15 2EU.

HSC *First Aid at Work Health and Safety (First Aid) Regulations (1981) and Approved Code of Practice* (HMSO, 1990).

Accommodation

DFE *Design Note 17, Guidelines for Environmental Design and Fuel Consumption in Educational Buildings.*

DFE *Building Bulletin 17, Craft design and technology accommodation in secondary schools* (1985), HMSO, ISBN 0 11 270562.

Asbestos

DFE Administrative Memorandum 3/86 *The Use of Asbestos in Educational Establishments*, issued to all schools in 1986. Further copies available from the Public Enquiry Unit, Department for Education, Sanctuary Buildings, Great Smith Street, London SW1P 3BT.

British Standards

BSI *Standards CATALOGUE*, British Standards Institute. A manufacturer or supplier of goods should be able to advise whether the goods meet the relevant British or European specifications or standards.

Ceramics

HSE *The Operation of Ceramic Kilns, Ceramic Industry Advisory Committee*, ISBN 0 71760630 9, price £6.50.

Institute of Materials (formerly the Institute of Ceramics) *Health and Safety in Ceramics: A Guide for Educational Workshops and Studios* (1991), ISBN 0 90 109242 8. Available from the Institute of Materials, 1 Carlton House Terrace, London SW1Y 5DP, price £6.00 plus £1.50 postage.

HSE *COSHH and the Production of Pottery: Approved Code of Practice* (COP 41), ISBN 0 11 885530 1, price £4.50.

BS6748 (1986) Specification for *Limits of Metal Release from Ceramic Ware, Glassware, Glass Ceramic Ware and Vitreous Enamel Ware.*

Control of substances hazardous to health (COSHH)

HSE COSHH *Subject Catalogue* (1990) free from HSE Books.

HSE COSHH: *Guidance for schools* (1989) ISBN 0 11 885511 5, price £2.00.

HSE *Control of Substances Hazardous to Health: Approved Codes of Practice* (HMSO 1989).

HSE *COSHH and the Production of Pottery Approved Code of Practice COP 41*, ISBN 0 11 885530 1, price £4.50.

Design

NAAIDT *Make it Safe! Safety Guidance for the Teaching of Design and Technology at Key Stages 1 and 2* (1992), ISBN 0 906457 07, price £3.50.

Display screen equipment

HSE *Health and Safety (Display Screen Equipment)* (1992) *Guidance on Regulations*, ISBN 0 71 760410 1, price £5.00.

Dust

HSC *Dust: general principles of protection* (1991), ISBN 0 11 885595 6, price £2.25.

Electrical equipment

The Electricity at Work Regulations (1989), (ST 1989/635) HMSO.

DFE *Building Bulletin 76 Maintenance of Electrical Services* (1992), ISBN 0 11 270799 8, price £13.50, available from HMSO.

HSC *Memorandum of Guidance on the Electricity at Work Regulations* (1989), ISBN 0 11 883963 2, price £4.00.

HSE *Guidance Note GS23 Electrical Safety in Schools* (1990), price £2.50.

HSC *The safe use of portable electrical apparatus: electrical safety* (1990), price £2.50.

HSE *Maintaining portable electric equipment in offices and other low risk environments*, ref Ind(g)160L, free leaflet from HSE Books.

HSE *Maintaining portable and transportable electrical equipment*, ISBN 0 71 760715 1, price £5.00.

Eye protection

BS 2092 (1987) *Specification for Eye-Protectors for Industrial and Non-Industrial Uses.*

Gas and flammable liquids

HSE *Storage and Use of Highly Flammable Liquids in Educational Establishments* (1986), (IAC/L15) free from HSE Books.

HSE leaflet *Gas Appliances - keep them serviced - keep them safe* (1994), (Ind(G)79(L)) free from HSE Books.

HSE *The keeping of liquefied petroleum gases (LPG) in cylinders and similar containers* (1986), ISBN 0 71 760631 7, price £3.25.

British Gas and DFE *Guidance Notes on Gas Safety in Educational Establishments* (1989), publication IM/25 available from British Gas plc, Service Engineering, 326 High Holborn, London WC1V 7PT.

Manual handling

HSE *Manual Handling Guidance on Regulations* (HMSO 1992), ISBN 0 71 760411 X, price £5.00.

Plastics

HSE *The application of COSHH to plastics processing* (1990), ISBN 0 11 885556 5, price £5.00.

Protective equipment

HSE *Personal Protective Equipment at Work Guidance on Regulations* (1992), ISBN 0 11 886334 7, price £5.00.

Safety signs

HSE leaflet *Signpost to the Safety Signs Regulations* (1994), free from HSE books.

Welding

HSE *Assessment of exposure to fumes from welding and allied processes Guidance Note EH 54* (1990), ISBN 0 11 885429 1, price £2.50.

HSE *The control of exposure to fumes from welding, brazing and similar processes: Guidance Note EH 54* (1990), ISBN 0 11 885439 9, price £2.50.

HSE *Welding and Flame-Cutting Guidance Note*, ISBN 0 11 883366 9, price £1.00.

Woodworking

HSE *Supervising for Safety in Woodworking* (1994), free booklet available from The Woodworking National Interest Group, HSE, 14 Cardiff Road, Luton, Bedfordshire LU1 1PP.

BS 4163 Code of Practice (1984) *Health and Safety in Workshops Schools and Similar Establishments.*

BS 5498 *Specification for the Safety of Hand Operated Cutting Machines* (1977).

BS 5304 *Safeguarding Machinery* (1975).

HSE *The Cutting Edge* leaflet and order form concerning safety in woodworking videos.

Work equipment

HSE *Work Equipment Guidance on Regulations* (HMSO 1992), ISBN 0 71 760414 4, price £5.00.

Workplace

HSC *Workplace Health, Safety and Welfare Approved Code of Practice* (HMSO 1992), ISBN 0 71 760413 6, price £5.00.

NAAIDT *Managing Health and Safety in School Workshops* (1992), ISBN 0 906457 08 04, price £7.50.

NAAIDT *Safety Training Courses for Teachers and Technicians Using School Workshops* (1991), ISBN 0 906457 06 8, price £10.00.

Addresses

British Standards Institution, Sales Department, 389 Chiswick High Road, London W4 4AL.

HSC and HSE booklets are available from Dillons Bookshops and Rymans Stores or HSE Books, PO Box 1999, Sudbury, Suffolk CO10 6FS. Telephone: 01787 313995.

HMSO publications are available from HMSO Publications, 49 High Holborn, London WC1U 6HB, or through any good bookseller.

NAAIDT (National Association of Advisers and Inspectors in Design and Technology), Honorary Secretary, 124 Kidmore Road, Caversham, Reading, Berkshire RG4 7NB. Telephone: 01734 233682.

NAAIDT publications are available from NAAIDT Publications, 16 Kingsway Gardens, Chandler's Ford, Hampshire SO5 1FE.

NSEAD (National Society for Education in Art and Design), The Gatehouse, Corsham, Wiltshire SN13 0B2. Telephone: 01249 716138.

9 Index

....

Printed in the United Kingdom for HMSO.
Dd.0300272, 5/95, C30, 3397/5, 5673, 322857.